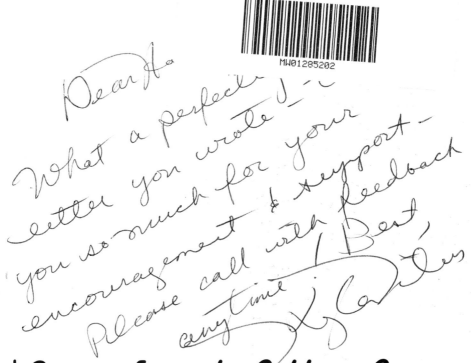

Secrets from the Cabbage Cove

**How to Create a New Millennium Superfood and Become
Less Dependent on the Food and Health Industries**

Copyright © 2015 Kyla M. Titus
All rights reserved.

Printed in the United States of America
ISBN-13: 978-1519689245
ISBN-10: 1519689241

Visit the Website: https://www.TheCabbageCove.com
Visit the Facebook page:
https://www.facebook.com/TheCabbageCove

Dedication

For my children

Grandchildren

And future generations

Table of Contents

Acknowledgments

Christina, Brenden and Dylan—for inspiring me to nurture through nature, not laboratories.

Richard Daley—for encouraging me to share my convictions.

Sue Butler—for becoming my third eye.

The Cabbage Cove customers—for expressing their delight and urging others to taste.

Foreword

I wrote this book because I felt I should share some secrets.

The secrets involve the knowledge I gained over three and a half decades of experience, self-education and common sense related to issues of food and health. I used this knowledge in growing, buying, preserving, preparing and serving healthy and delicious food to my family, friends and customers.

What I learned did not evolve easily for me. I struggled through mountains of mainstream misinformation on diet and health. Because of so much conflicting, confusing information, I was not able to avoid many harmful medical and dental procedures, medications and dietary difficulties. There was a serious lack of accurate guidelines, but I was determine to self-educate in order to provide best practices for my family. I am somewhat encouraged that today there exists wider availability of organic and less complex foods; however, I feel there still is much reformation needed in the food and health industries.

My hope is that readers can learn from my experience and not only avoid trial and error with their diets and health, but experience a positive modification—if not life-altering—to the unhealthy, de-energizing, hyper-flavored, expensive, unnatural and dehumanizing food industry upon which we have become so dependent.

In addition, I hope I help readers realize they need to use their own intelligence and effort in deciphering this food industry (and its government bedfellow) propaganda and understand that everything in life is political—right down to the choices made every single day in food selection, storage, preparation and consumption.

There is one important "secret" I must share first because of my strong conviction it is central to any discussion on diet and health. It is not really a secret at all, except that for so many reasons so many people ignore it. It is such a simple concept that it truly astounds me that we need contemplate it at all:

Grow, buy, preserve, prepare, serve and eat only REAL food.

We need to start with this simple concept and avoid anything that scientists create in a laboratory. This includes preservatives, flowing agents, colorings, etc.—anything that does not occur in nature, whenever we can. Think about how ridiculous it is that this ever needs to be said here, or anywhere else.

In my view, we are currently undergoing a mass experiment of the kind we have never before faced in human history—consuming genetically modified organisms (or

GMOs). I am a firm believer in consuming whole, unadulterated and unaltered foods only. However, if altered foods continue to be offered, then I believe they need to be properly and honestly described on labels. Currently, there are pitifully few laws requiring GMO disclosure, so without self-education consumers do not know what they are buying. There are many people who feel consuming these "Frankenfoods" could affect human and other life drastically in generations to come. Certainly I reject biotech industries and their government cronies' sales pitch spin that there is no "discernable" difference between a GMO and a non-GMO; however, even if others do not, I believe we all have a right to at least know what we are buying.

Industry has spent millions of dollars lobbying Congress to prevent GMO labeling laws in addition to fighting grassroots ballot initiative efforts, and to date they have been quite successful across the United States.[1] Therefore, another companion secret to the above is:

Learn how to decipher food and drug labels.[2]

Deciphering these labels takes quite a bit of practice, but if consumers desire processed foods yet want to avoid GMOs, they need to spend the time learning the names of those ingredients that are derivatives or questioning those they do not recognize—because there are many of them. For example,

---

[1] GMO industry giants have lobbied furiously for no labeling laws because of their admitted fear that if a product is labeled GMO, consumers would not buy it.

[2] The Non-GMO Project organization is independently verifying products that claim to be GMO-free. The labels on these products bear the seal "Non-GMO Project Verified," and is currently consumers' most reliable information for foods that do not bear the "USDA Organic" seal.

dextrose, polydextrose, dextrin, maltodextrin, citrate, citric acid and modified food starch are just a few common ones that industry derives from GMO corn. Wending one's way through some ingredient lists can be quite a chore. Unfortunately, the old tenet of avoiding products with ingredient names you cannot pronounce is not enough anymore, because of the shameful lack of GMO labeling laws nationwide. For example, high fructose corn syrup is easy to pronounce, but the name does not indicate it is an altered product.[3]

Many corporate and government entities cite scientific studies as reason for public compliance and acceptance of industrial and laboratory food. However, the public must begin to think for themselves and reject that knowing something is exclusive to modern science only. We can gain knowledge through other means, such as experience, common sense and an open mind. Many food and health industry agents disagree vehemently, citing their science as the absolute standard of knowledge, but over time it seems to me these assertions come from a standpoint of maintaining control over people and their wallets rather than proving through scientific methods that something is true.

The mass use of unnatural food is only one part of why I feel our food and health systems need revision. Another reason is that what we think we know about diet and health is so highly controlled by industry that we have lost the ability to

---

[3] Criticism of HFCS has been widespread and thankfully sales have dropped dramatically. However, industry is answering back by attempting to rename the same product (so ignorant common folk will start buying it again). So the term "corn sugar" is being adopted and the industry argument is that "a sugar is a sugar." However, whether called HFCS, corn sugar or anything else, this substance is still a GMO. Further, without proper labeling these products will continue to sell and the public will remain uninformed.

rely on our own natural instinct regarding food choices. We incorrectly believe that because as laypeople we cannot decode industry, scientific or political jargon, we must blindly follow the recommendations of those who can. We have allowed industry to rule our lives in every aspect, and in the process have lost respect for our environment, community, elders and the art of living. But guess what? You can create your own language of living, and great change can result.

Consider the organic foods movement. Many people ridiculed my lengthy travel and sometimes great expense in seeking out organics for my family during a time when very few were readily available. Despite these obstacles, there was no doubt in my mind that someday fresh, organic produce would become available in virtually every supermarket across the country if enough people voted for it with their dollars. I am happy to see this vision materialize, and I am glad for my contribution.

Similarly, I feel I can effect change with this book by sharing my secrets on how to create a superfood for the new millennium—one that I hope will eventually see far more organically-naturally-locally grown real foods and far less GMO-chemical-nanotech[4] substances available for mass consumption. If you agree this is an ideal for which to strive, then I hope this book will help you to effect change too.

Thank you for reading, and may these secrets serve you well![5]

---

[4] Nanotechnology refers to the manipulation of the tiniest particles, such as atoms and molecules.

[5] A disclaimer is necessary in case someone asserts that following some advice herein somehow caused harm or determines there is a litigious opportunity

because I failed to provide one. Therefore, if you are under a doctor's care for any medical condition whatsoever, please consult with him or her before making any lifestyle/dietary changes.

The basis of this book is my opinion only. I make no health claims whatsoever. In fact, I do not claim I know anything absolutely. However, the side effects of reading on include learning how to create a new millennium superfood, whether you live in the woods, on a farm, in the suburbs or in a city apartment, becoming at least somewhat freer from dependence upon the food and health conglomerates and saving an awful lot of money. My recommendation is to use common sense, do your own research and proceed at your own risk of improving your life.

Introduction

There is a food with so much potential for enabling people to take more control over their own lives in so many ways that it is astounding it is not available in every supermarket across the nation. What is this transformative "new millennium superfood?" Readers may suspect it has something to do with cabbage, and they would be correct. However, what transforms this already extraordinarily healthy vegetable into a superfood is this—the process of fermentation and the resultant boost in probiotics, coupled with this book's unique ways of creating and using it.

What is fermentation? Simply, it is a process that turns sugars present in various substances into either acids through the action of bacteria, or alcohol through the action of yeasts. It is a natural biological process that humans have cultivated for thousands of years.

Although the art of fermentation has been around for a while, the ideas and recipes in this book are so new and exciting they have turned even cabbage haters into diehard Cabbage Cove enthusiasts. Many customers who stated they do not like cabbage or sauerkraut are amazed at how much they like these varieties of fermented cabbage. Most people do not recognize Cabbage Cove ferments as anything they have tasted or used before.

It is the enthusiasm and surprise of so many upon tasting my creations that inspired me to share my secrets in a book. Learn about what to do with cabbage—one of the healthiest and most versatile vegetables on Earth. Learn how to boost your levels of health and energy in a matter of days and create ultra-healthy meals quickly—whether preparing a snack or a candlelit dinner. Learn how to save hundreds of dollars or more per month on your food bill alone, and so much more than that on unnecessary treatments, drugs and beauty products. Learn how to grow a superfood easily whether living on a country farm or a city apartment. My hope is that within the pages of this book I have given readers a way to eat and live more naturally without retreating from modern life. Rather, people may become adaptable enough to make a significant difference in their lives in the new millennium.

In this book, I will be discussing a little bit of science and a lot of the art involved in creating a new millennium superfood that is so healthy, delicious, energizing, timesaving, versatile, inexpensive, ecological and empowering, I can hardly believe that so few people are aware of its life-altering potential. Through my creative application of this ancient culinary craft, a completely new way of approaching your diet is possible.

I have developed a way of turning plain fermented cabbage into something that you will not only eat, but will enjoy eating immensely. Surprisingly, after only a few short days, your body will begin to crave it. Regardless of lifestyle or socioeconomic status, adding these ferments to your diet is so easy and inexpensive you will wonder what took everyone so long in rediscovering this amazing ancient process.

Thankfully, the benefits of adding probiotics to our diets through fermented foods have gained attention. There are many books on the subject of fermentation, and I encourage you to discover them as well. You can ferment many different foods, but here we discuss only cabbage, arguably the world's most perfect food to ferment, coming ready-made with all the ingredients necessary for success, without using a "starter."[6]

This book will discuss the qualities of raw fermented cabbage that make it a superfood. It will explain the Where, What and How of making your own, as well as include recipe ideas that will surprise and delight you, some of which come from the Cabbage Cove's enthusiastic customers. There is additional space for your own recipes, because the product and process encourage culinary creativity.

The last chapter offers some "unsolicited" advice on complimenting a raw fermented foods lifestyle. It includes some simple natural remedies and recommendations—what I consider the most tried and true ones. These too follow this book's mantra of easy and inexpensive.

Finally, there is a note on the Cabbage Cove, which was created due to urgings of many people who had awestruck reaction to the ferments. Many of them first learned about them as a side dish in a restaurant. People began to ask if they could take some home and use in their own kitchens. Soon people came to the restaurant just to buy the ferments. What

---

[6] A starter is a culture rich in microorganisms that was grown specifically for the purpose of adding to foods in order to ensure fermentation.

was surprising was how little most people knew about fermented cabbage and its probiotic benefits. What they did know was how tasty and versatile it was.

This book will help people understand just how important it is to include raw, fresh fermented foods—in particular cabbage—to their diets. If they try the methods and ideas presented here, they will surely find some way to incorporate this superfood into their lifestyle. People may email thecabbagecove@hotmail.com or visit the Facebook page www.facebook.com/thecabbagecove with any questions, shared experiences, creative recipes (which may be added to this work if desired) and especially to share ways in which the information has helped make a change in their lives.

And it will.

1 A New Millennium Superfood

Healthful

"Finish your vegetables" is a battle cry of many a parent, and with good reason. It is common knowledge that most vegetables contain highly beneficial vitamins, minerals, fiber, oils and micronutrients while being low in calories and fat. There is currently a long list of studies that credit vegetable nutrients with disease-fighting properties—including cancer and heart disease—and that list is continually growing. However, vegetable preparation method is of utmost importance—or the benefits are lost.

As the lead member of the cruciferous family of vegetables, which also includes broccoli, cauliflower and Brussels sprouts, cabbage is  particularly healthful. It is especially high in Vitamins C and K, high in Vitamin B6 and folate and a very good source of many other nutrients. Now, take fresh, raw cabbage and ferment it, and this vegetable that is incredibly healthful to start is transformed into a probiotic-rich, low-carb, vegetarian-vegan, gluten-free "superfood."

Very simply, this is because the process of fermentation creates an environment that helps beneficial microorganisms—commonly known as "probiotics"—proliferate, while it eliminates harmful ones. These "good bacteria" take up residence in our guts, improve digestion, aid in elimination of waste, boost the immune system, keep harmful bacteria at bay, and much more. Continuing research discovers more benefits to consuming probiotics every day.

Several Cabbage Cove customers have indicated success with their life-long problems of digestive difficulties, after only a short time on fresh, raw fermented cabbage. Traditional medications, dietary changes and even surgeries proved futile in their quest for relief. However, the addition of probiotic-rich Cabbage Cove ferments to their diets helped when all else failed.

The improvement of digestion is the first, most noticeable health benefit when consuming probiotics; however, do not assume a food traditionally rich in probiotics comes that way in supermarkets. If eating one of these foods does not help, then the source may not contain viable probiotics. In order to receive the maximum benefit and recognize results it is crucial to:

Eat only fresh, raw fermented cabbage.

One of the few negative side effects of eating raw cabbage people cite is accompanying bloating and gas; however, these effects do not occur for most people when eating raw fermented cabbage. Think of any fermented product as being predigested, and it will be easy to understand that many digestive difficulties could be minimized if not eliminated.

Many people cook cabbage, and while this may reduce bloating and gas to a degree, it comes with the price of loss of valuable nutrients. Fermented cabbage is not heated so there is far less loss of vitamins and minerals.

Another negative some cite is that raw cabbage contains slightly higher sugar content than most other green leafy vegetables. This should really not be a concern, because most of the sugars are indigestible by humans, but quite digestible by beneficial bacteria.

In fact, cabbage comes ready made with all the qualities and ingredients necessary to become a superfood through the process of fermentation. It is the perfect compromise between eating either raw or cooked cabbage.[7] In addition, although many other foods may be fermented, none is so easy to transform and as healthy as cabbage.

Another point to make in this section is that a lot of new attention is being given to what are called "prebiotics." While probiotics refer to the microorganisms themselves, prebiotics refer to substances that help probiotics thrive. Good sources of prebiotics include berries, onions, garlic, sweet potatoes, asparagus and whole wheat,[8] among many others. There is plenty of information on prebiotics available online, and it may be wise to include some in the diet along with foods rich in probiotics.

What about supplementation? Many people take probiotics in pill form, and certainly this is better than not if no foods rich in them are available. However:

The best way to benefit from any dietary essential is to consume it in its natural state.

---

[7] Other vegetables can be fermented too and produce similar results, but a starter is usually necessary for main ingredients other than cabbage.
[8] Which of course can also be fermented as in sourdough bread. The pre-digestion of wheat through the action of microorganisms may help some people who have sensitivities to wheat.

Believe it or not, modern science does not have all the answers and new symbiotic relationships and substances are discovered every day. Why not simply trust the whole food?

Our "gut flora"—indeed all our biological components—are under such attack every day that it is especially important we consume plenty of both pro- and pre-biotics. The assault comes from so many aspects of modern life: overuse of antibiotics and other prescription and non-prescription drugs; household and other chemicals in our environment; GMO, nanotech and chemically altered foods and the denatured soil in which they grow; electro-magnetic fields and radiation; sedentary lifestyles; lack of sunshine; the stress of modern life...the barrage seems endless.

A word about antibiotics. While a life-saving and valuable medical tool when used properly, they are literally not to be taken lightly. First, through their overuse we are creating "superbugs" for which there are no medical cures. Only the strongest immune systems will be able to combat this onslaught, and in modern society, these are in the minority.

Second, without the protection of probiotics, many people enter a cycle of repeated antibiotic use, reinfection and weakening immune system. With each reinfection a stronger variety of antibiotics will usually be prescribed. However, a stronger, more resistant variety of bacteria usually answers this strategy, and so the cycle continues. If this pattern sounds familiar, it is because it happens so frequently.

If this cycle begins, it must be stopped immediately. Cease taking all drugs, if a fever develops allow it rather than block it, immediately add a high-quality probiotic supplement with as many varieties of bacteria as possible and incorporate pro- and pre-biotic foods in the diet every day from that day forward for the lifetime. Work with the body's natural processes, not against them and restoration of good health will be more easily attainable.

Most indications are that our gut health plays perhaps the most important role in shoring up our immune systems and preventing disease. Some estimates of the role probiotics play in boosting our immune systems reach better than 90 percent. There is more than just mounting modern scientific evidence of their importance. There are the thousands of years of human experience with fermentation of all kinds of foods. However, as a society we have lost this art in favor of modern industrial and technological lifestyles. We are removed from nature and its processes, and self-sufficiency and the homegrown/homemade-food void has been quickly filled by the food and health industrial complex.

As with any nutrient, it is far better to consume it in its natural state than to isolate it from its symbiotic relationships. However, be aware that some foods traditionally rich in probiotics, for example sauerkraut and yogurt, are usually not beneficial in commercial varieties found in supermarkets. Many manufacturers pasteurize or include additives that kill bacteria. Even careful label reading does not guarantee results. In addition many of these foods travel hundreds even thousands of miles. In general, the farther the food travels to its consumer, the less healthful it is.

The best way to enjoy the health benefits of probiotics is to learn the art of fermentation and produce the food in the home kitchen from fresh, locally grown, preferably organic raw cabbage. It does not matter whether the kitchen is in a farmhouse, a cabin in the woods, a house in the suburbs or a city apartment. If preferred, seek out local sources of ferments if you can, but make sure what you purchase is fresh and raw. Otherwise there will be no probiotic health benefit.

Delicious

One reason the parental battle cry mentioned above is so recognizable involves the issue of taste. Many American children just do not seem to like their vegetables. Part of the reason involves the surrendering en masse of home processed, fresh vegetables in favor of industrialized processed foods. Children were and still are served un-fresh vegetables, often canned, over salted, overcooked and devoid of nutrients. Concomitantly, their palates have been corrupted by extreme and artificial flavors deliberately pushed on them by food conglomerates in order to cause addiction, thereby creating lifelong consumers of their products. Finally, for generations there has been a lack of availability of fresh, raw fermented foods and the accompanying health benefits and unique flavors they offer.

American palates have been radically altered away from natural preferences. However, the techniques and recipes developed over decades that are presented in this book result in such new and delicious ways to enjoy the ancient staple of fermented cabbage that people with average palates tasting it for the first time are amazed. Even people who claim they do not like cabbage are surprised by its deliciousness. In fact, some have asserted an actual hatred of cabbage, and if brave enough to have tried a sampling are astounded. Many have claimed that to them it does not even taste like cabbage. Yes, there are even ways to get children to eat it willingly.

The secret regarding flavor was to:

Create something for everyone based on flavors of cuisines with which many may already enjoy and be familiar.

It does the person who hates cabbage or sauerkraut no good to offer them raw, fermented plain cabbage, despite its health benefits. They simply will not eat it unless it is delicious to them and unlike any cabbage they have tasted before. Therefore, the Cabbage Cove recipes were developed with the purpose of tasting far better than any fermented cabbage or sauerkraut most people have tried, in very recognizable and delicious flavors.

Readers might ask themselves if there is at least one variety among the following list they would be willing to try: Cajun, Cinnamon, Garlic & Ginger, Garlic & Herb, German, Ginger & Lime, Greek, Horseradish, Indian, Italian, Japanese, Korean, Lemon Bay, Lemon & Pepper, Mexican, Plain, Spicy, Thai or Ukrainian. Most assuredly their answer would be "yes." All of these varieties are 100 percent ferment, with the particular fresh vegetables, herbs and spices added to the cabbage mixture before the miraculous transformation begins. The result is totally unique, incomparably delicious flavors that cannot be duplicated by combining the same ingredients unfermented.

Another very important secret involves texture:

Finely chop cabbage instead of shredding it.

The Cabbage Cove does not shred its cabbage, as most recipes for fermented cabbage or sauerkraut call for, it chops it finely. This idea originated from a desire to make the product more palatable to children—and it does. However, many adults also prefer the finer texture to that of traditional sauerkraut. This, coupled with the wonderful new flavors, makes Cabbage Cove fresh, raw fermented cabbage a concentrated delicacy.

Energizing

Different civilizations around the world have been fermenting cabbage for thousands of years. Certainly the discovery of the wonderful flavor would be reason enough to continue the practice. However, without modern scientists guiding them, did they know this was a health maintaining and boosting food? Almost certainly, and not because of any scientific analysis, but simply because of the way it makes a person feel. The most amazing thing happens when regularly incorporating fresh, raw fermented cabbage into a diet—in a short time energy levels rapidly increase and there is an accompanying lightness of being—and of belly. This of course presumes there is no gross concurrent consumption of something counterproductive.

In fact, these ferments feel very filling yet can even be eaten before exercising without ill effect. Indeed, after eating a very small amount, many report feeling immediately energized. After sampling the cinnamon variety, one customer actually shouted that it made her feel like dancing. Ingredients such as hot peppers, fresh ginger and fresh garlic in some varieties not only wake up the taste buds but stimulate and protect the whole system.

Adding these ferments to a diet reduces the desire for larger amounts of food, thereby reducing total caloric intake. This coupled with an almost immediate increase in energy should result in:

Weight loss and an overall increase in levels of health.

Fast

Once this unique fermented cabbage is made or purchased, it is a snap to create fast and easy snacks, appetizers, salads and meals by simply scooping a small portion out of a jar with a spoon or fork. Nothing could be faster. In fact many people report they just eat a few bites right out of the jar when in a hurry, and hunger is satisfied.

Smooth a bit on a lettuce leaf and roll it up for a quick snack. Add any leftover veggies or pieces of cheese or meat to the lettuce and make an instant lettuce sandwich. Add a dollop to a hot dog or hamburger for a totally new taste. In fact, with so many varieties available, a hot dog could taste different every day for weeks. Chop some lettuce, place in bowl and place a scoop on top and an instant salad has been created. There is no need to add dressing either as these ferments are so flavorful and so moist. Serve a scoop with any meal and instantly transform it into a gourmet one, worthy of candlelight and fine wine.

Because these recipes result in a product that is so concentrated—both in density and flavor—a little goes a long way. Pack a little in a small bag or container. There is no need for refrigeration—it can be taken anywhere and added to anything or simply eaten on its own. The reason this wonderful fresh, raw fermented cabbage is also a fast-food is because:

All the chopping, preparation and seasoning has been done beforehand.

In addition, depending on how quickly it is used, it can be kept out on the counter at room temperature so there is no need to heat it up (which could destroy good bacteria as well as nutrients). However, even when refrigerated all that is necessary to warm it is to place it in cooled but still warm pan juices or press or mix it into warm (not hot) food.

Versatile

There are so many ways to use the fermented cabbage described in this book, and more are sure to develop once the process is mastered. Not only is this product healthy, delicious and time-saving, it can be used to compliment just about any favorite food. The process encourages creativity, so readers who learn how to make it themselves will surely find new ways of using it in addition to developing their own favorite flavors.

All varieties compliment any meat. Use any fresh, uncooked variety as you would sauerkraut on hot dogs, pork, hamburgers, veal, chicken, turkey, sausage and fish. Experiment with different varieties and different meats or meat substitutes for unique and flavorful combinations. Although cooking will destroy some of the health benefits, it can also be added in the cooking process for flavors' sake, and a whole new world of uses will be unveiled. Remember, even if the probiotics are destroyed in cooking, there are still the benefits of consuming a predigested food, saving a lot of time and enjoying the marvelous flavors in a new way.

All varieties also compliment any vegetable. Whatever the favorite vegetables are, instant flavor can be added to wake them up. Add to chopped lettuce for an instant salad. Sautéing fresh green beans in a little butter and garlic? Skip chopping the garlic and mix the Garlic & Herb variety into the pan juices after the heat is off and the pan has cooled a little. Mash a scoop of the Mexican variety with a baked potato or sweet potato for instant stuffed potatoes. Replace the breading with the Italian variety for delicious stuffed mushrooms. The possibilities are endless.

One of the Cabbage Cove's favorite uses of the ferments is pairing it with different cheeses for spectacular appetizers and meals. For example, use feta with the Greek variety, mozzarella with the Italian or Swiss cheese with the German. Again, use the imagination and the possibilities are endless. One customer uses the scoop variety of tortilla chips, melts small pieces of cheese inside them in a low oven and then places a dollop of complimentary fermented cabbage variety on top.

There is even a cinnamon variety the Cabbage Cove offers that is called a "dessert" variety. To the delight and surprise of customers (who have been brave enough to try it), this variety can be mixed with plain vanilla ice cream, adding a cinnamon flavor and a crunch that is similar to walnuts while cutting the calories in half. Or put the cinnamon variety by itself in a small bowl, add some chopped fruits, nuts and a sweetener of choice for an instant probiotic rich, low-carb, low-cal, gluten-free breakfast "cereal."

The secret is that:

This product truly can be used with any meat, fish, vegetable, eggs, grain, dairy product or even dessert.

Inexpensive

Prices of cabbage fluctuate of course, but at anywhere from 40 to 90 cents per pound, depending on climate and season, this is a far superior economic choice for healthful and delicious sustenance than expensive supplements and empty-yet-high calorie processed food. One and a half pounds should produce about a quart of concentrated ferment, about 30 ounces.

If one ounce is considered a serving, then for a couple who uses three servings per day one quart would last them five days and:

The cost in cabbage is about a dollar for a whole quart and about three cents per serving.

This is a critical issue in the new millennium, when most Americans continue to experience not only skyrocketing food costs, but lowering wages as well. The Cabbage Cove hopes to offer a way to combat this trend by teaching people how to take control of their palates, their health, their time and their pocketbooks by employing the ancient and natural art of fermenting cabbage.

At these prices, even impoverished people can fight back and regain their minds, bodies and resources. The food and health conglomerates and their bedfellow politicians want people to remain addicted and compliant to the current food system, because profits are substantial. Very cheap (in every sense), unnatural food is produced and passed off as sustenance—and an obscene amount of money is charged for it.[9] However, with the proper approach and a few dollars, anyone can easily help themselves improve their health and economic statuses.

Of course, there are other costs to making fresh, raw fermented cabbage, including a possible initial cost for supplies. However, once those minimal supplies are purchased there is very little else besides cabbage, fresh vegetables and herbs, and some spices if desired, that is required.

Green

Many aspects of the modern food paradigm as it relates to our environment are of concern in the new millennium. The industrialization and centralization of our food supply takes a heavy toll on our resources. Massive amounts of resources, such as electricity and water, are consumed in production, massive amounts of byproducts/waste are in need of disposal and massive amounts of product needs to be shipped across the United States.

When producing fermented cabbage in the home, resources such as electricity and water are not even needed.

Fermenters may choose to use, say, a food processor, but it is not necessary as cabbage can be chopped using good old-fashioned muscle power and a sharp knife. Lighting would

---

[9] In addition, many of these unnatural foods are subsidized heavily by taxpayer dollars.

only be necessary at night or in a very dark kitchen. There is no need for a stove or microwave oven. Even water is not absolutely necessary if fermenting in a very warm, high humidity environment.

There is virtually no waste in home fermentation.

Most of the equipment is reusable, there is no slick, shiny product packaging that ends up in landfills and the ferments can last for a very long time if not used immediately. Produce trimmings can and should go into a home compost system, a garden or to any animals that may enjoy them.

Shipping over vast distances is economically, nutritionally and environmentally expensive.

We pay for the cost of shipping in the price of our food, the depletion of nutrients in produce that is not consumed as soon after harvest as possible and the effect on the environment from carbon emissions and stress on our infrastructures, among others. People on the East Coast of the United States should simply not be purchasing produce from the West Coast, and vice versa. The closer to home a family's food comes from, the better. Ideally, much of it will come from a home garden, a local farm or farmers' market and/or a market whose management principles include buying local. If people care about their money, their health and their environment they can change this industrial food model drastically by relying on a little ingenuity, a lot of local food sources and some of the ideas in this book.

Another important secret belonging in this section that seems to elude even some food safety experts is that:

Fermented cabbage is a food preservation method all on its own.

It does not require refrigeration or any other method that consumes energy, such as canning.[10] This is because with just the right amount of salt added to the cabbage the bad bacteria die and the good remain. The beneficial bacteria further protect the food by producing byproducts that drastically lower the pH (creating an acid environment) in which any undesirable bacteria newly introduced cannot survive. As long as there is something available in the mix for our friendly probiotics to consume, they will continue to reduce or maintain the low pH of the environment, and the food does not need to be refrigerated.

Nor do we need or want to rely on modern food safety's chemical sterility. Nature can supply all the food safety we need—if we learn to work with it and not against it. Current food safety regulations for commercial food processors, as well as the mindsets of many household ones, often require or include chemical sterilization of kitchens. This stems from our societal germ phobia, which exists for many reasons, both real and imagined. Mass media support of this phobia includes advertising campaigns designed to convince us we need certain products in our lives. Common household products contain dangerous toxins that are absorbed by our skin and breathed into our lungs on a daily basis. Medical products such

---

[10] Many people think the Cabbage Cove's products are pickled or canned. This is not so. The high heat involved in the canning process would destroy valuable probiotics, thereby working against the whole purpose of fermentation, which is to provide tremendous health benefits through the consumption of our friendly bacteria. In addition, when speaking of energy, the canning process also requires the use of gas, electricity or wood in order to boil water.

as antibiotics create internal sterility and result in resistant bacteria and weakened immune systems. We are so fearful of germs that an arsenal full of dangerous chemicals and pharmaceuticals concocted by industry is available everywhere—for a price, of course, and one that is not just economic.

Another important concern in the new millennium not only involves what types of resources to use in order to supply energy in the form of electricity, but whether we can keep our grids safe from sabotage. Well, if a grid fails for any reason, whether accidental or intentional, the household with raw fermented cabbage bubbling on its countertop will have fresh vegetables available for weeks—potentially months depending on where it is stored—without refrigeration, whereas the household without will only have fresh food available for a few days.

Empowering

As more control over their food sources is established, people will begin to understand that relying on mass media, food industry and big government for their food and health information may not always be what is best for them or our planet. These sources can be unreliable, if not untrustworthy, because individual and local community empowerment is not the objective. Guess what is?

A food substance that restores or maintains health, protects against illness, tastes delicious, energizes, easily fits into a busy lifestyle, can be used in hundreds of different ways, is incredibly inexpensive and helps reduce stress on our environment does exist—and it is empowering. It was developed by nature and nurtured by people who observed and worked with nature, not against it. Now, more than ever, this low-tech, high-value sustenance desperately needs to be introduced into the modern kitchen because:

It can help free families from dependence on big farms and big pharma that has grown exponentially over generations now.

As we moved farther away from the places where food grows, we became more detached from our environment and more dependent on centralized food industry. We have forgotten what our farm families taught us and placed our faith in strangers to provide us with health-sustaining foods. Unfortunately, many of those upon whom we rely do not always have our health and well-being best interests at heart.

What we may not realize is that we can take back control over our food and grow our own—even if we live in the cities. The simple instructions in this book will help people create something enormously beneficial in their own kitchens, and if the system takes hold and becomes a routine part of a fermented foods lifestyle, far less denatured food and drugs will be consumed and superior health and quality of life can be established.

It can place more economic resources into individual households and local communities.

Not only will far less health-damaging food be consumed with a fermented foods lifestyle, far less money will be spent with its maintenance. If a system and a routine are established, very quickly there will be a feeling of self-reliance that will develop.

This leads to self-sustaining motivation with the creation of every bubbling, living batch—as well as with every dollar that is saved.

It can help combat food addiction, so that food choices become naturally more healthful.

When something tastes so delicious and like nothing has tasted before, people will generally eat and continue to eat it. As fresh, raw fermented cabbage in all the varieties a person can imagine are joyfully added to typical snacks and meals, there will come a desire for more of this and less of the ultra-sweet and chemically laden snack and processed foods that are deliberately designed to hook people. Over a short time, the palate will be retrained and people may find themselves choosing more salads over French fries in restaurants, coffee, tea or water over soda or fruit juice at the snack bar or a hot dog with a scoop of the fermented cabbage (that was perhaps neatly packed into a purse or pocket) over a slice of pizza.

It can reduce and/or eliminate the need for expensive supplements or drugs, and as health is restored and there is less illness, far less time and money will be spent supporting a sick healthcare system.

When considering the cost of food, many people do not think of the outrageous medical care cost of poor food choices to not only them, but their communities and societies as well. For those who do consider it however, there is a question as to whether or not they are receiving the correct information. Those alive in the 20th and 21st centuries have witnessed ever-changing food and drug recommendations, which is really quite remarkable given that knowledge derived through modern science is touted by its minions as superior to indigenous or folk knowledge. A person might even come to believe that dietary recommendations change more often due to food industry and profit desires than scientific facts, when one year we are told not to eat saturated fat, for example, and then the next year we are. Most laypeople can think of many examples of this "scientific seesaw."

Perhaps the answers are simpler than we have been led to believe in modern life. Scientific knowledge is usually gained through theory and by dissecting something and analyzing its parts. Common or folk knowledge is usually gained through experience and by observing the whole natural event. With the former, only a few trained in their own language and systems can decipher the process, and if that process is held to the highest standard in a society, then the "uneducated" masses have no input (read power). With the latter, all people can be involved and only their individual perspectives could affect a deviation from common understanding. However:

The power in understanding is their own, not someone else's.

Yes, fresh, raw fermented cabbage is an empowering food. Not only can home fermenters decide what goes into their food, they can help change the food and health systems because as bodies become healthier, minds do too. As they become more self-reliant and less apt to robotic response to media, commercial or big government interests, their thinking could change because they will experience first-hand, in their own kitchens something miraculous. Then they may make one of the most political decisions any average person can make— where and on what to spend their money.

2 *The Where*

The Kitchen

Truly any kitchen can be used to ferment cabbage. In fact, a kitchen is not even required. Any space where cabbage can be prepared, mixed and packed will work. Counter space is needed primarily for chopping cabbage and other vegetables, mixing chopped ingredients together and then packing the finished product into jars; therefore, a fair amount of space is required. If counter space is limited, a small folding table can be retrieved from a closet and set up easily.

Contrary to popular belief, the kitchen does not need to be chemically sterilized. Chemicals and other dangerous substances and emissions are pervasive throughout our lives, in our living spaces, carpets, furniture, walls, floors, appliances, clothes, drapery, cosmetics and more. These products are creating all sorts of health problems, including slow and painful, or sometimes quick, death. Currently, there is very little we can do to eliminate the entire toxic load of chemicals we are exposed to everyday; however, we may be able to reduce our load to a degree. Certainly we can choose not to further add to it by purchasing and using dangerous commercial chemical cleaning supplies for use in an already toxic environment.

This discussion is necessary in general, but in particular because chemical sterilization of our cooking utensils, equipment, water and surfaces can work against the fermentation process, so another very important secret is:

Do not use chemical cleaners to "sterilize" the kitchen when preparing cabbage for fermentation.

Remember, we do not want to kill the good bacteria, only the bad. Sterilization for our purposes then involves minimizing the bad bacteria and shoring up the good. This is accomplished by adding just the right amount of natural salt (not processed table salt) to the cabbage, which our beneficial organisms can tolerate but most undesirables cannot.

Begin with clean, but not chemically sterile, surfaces. If rinsing or washing ingredients is desired then a sink would be helpful; however, be careful if the water source contains high amounts of antibacterial agents, such as sulfur or chlorine. Again, too much sterilization and the ferments may fail. If anyone feels averse to continuing without some sort of sterilization, instead of spraying chemicals on surfaces and into the air, use mild, non-antibacterial soap and water, boil equipment and/or use white distilled vinegar on surfaces.

Equipment and Supplies

Recommended equipment and supplies include:

- Large mixing bowl(s): necessary for measuring chopped cabbage, using as a vehicle for moisture extraction of freshly chopped cabbage and for thorough mixing of cabbage with other ingredients.

- Small countertop scale to five or 10 pounds with ounces clearly marked: necessary for determining the right amount of salt to mix into freshly chopped cabbage.

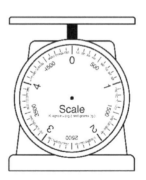

- Glass Mason jars, lids and bands (wide mouth preferred): necessary for packing, fermenting and storage—quart size recommended but pint size can be used as effectively.

- Food processor (optional): not necessary but certainly a very useful time-saving tool for finely chopping cabbage and other vegetables and herbs.

- pH paper, range 0-6 (optional): not necessary but useful if unsure about the developing product, although bubbling and gas buildup indicate success just as well. Most ferments' pH fall below 4.0 in a few days and continue falling as the fermentation process continues. (To put the numbers in perspective, most state health regulations require refrigeration of food items with pH levels above 4.5.)

- Cutting board(s), various large and small knives: essential even if using food processor; cabbage needs to be chopped into manageable pieces for food processor bowl, vegetables need to be chopped, shredded or diced as needed and herbs are generally better chopped with a large chef's knife than in a food processor.

- Various utensils for measuring, mixing and packing: a long-handled, hard plastic pasta spoon is an amazing utensil for this process as it can be used to mix, scoop and pack—the handle can even be used to release air bubbles from jars if it is unpadded and thin enough. Make sure it is made of hard plastic and has teeth. Measuring spoons and a two- or four-cup glass measure are essential.

Other utensils that may be helpful include spatula scrapers, spoons and Mason jar funnels. (Make sure no metal utensils are used to pack or touch the glass jars.)

The Fermentation Space

Of greater importance than preparation space is the temperature and humidity of the space in which the cabbage will ferment. The temperature should not be too warm or an inferior product with a shorter life span will result, and the humidity should not be too low or the product will dry out and fermentation could fail.

In general, fermentation will occur at room temperature or below, and above freezing. The warmer the temperature, the faster fermentation will occur, and the cooler the temperature the slower it will occur. The speed of fermentation is relative to the temperature. The ideal range is between 65 and 72 degrees Fahrenheit, as this will produce a very fine product in a relatively short time. In addition, keep the product away from direct sunlight or a very bright sunlit room as this might affect the temperature.

Adding brine should help keep the product moist enough, but awareness of the climate and season should be of note when choosing a fermentation space. Very dry climates and wintertime heat may dry out the top layer if enough brine is not added. If the color or any other major differences between the top and bottom layers occur, the top layer can simply be removed (however, ideally the whole batch is retained).

Another factor in choosing a fermentation space is the event known as "heaving." Jars should be "burped" every day, and at some point within a few days, either when burping or all on its own, the ferment in all its glory may let loose a gush of gas and liquid that could bubble over the sides of the jar. Therefore, some protection is recommended underneath the jars. Old pans or cookies sheets lined with old towels work well (of course, these should be cleaned in between batches). Burping can also be done over a sink if heaving is suspected as being imminent, for example if the jar band becomes hard to open or the lid looks puckered. Watching the product heave is one of the great joys of fermenting because it indicates viability and therefore success. In addition, the aroma is wonderful and begs an immediate taste of the product.

The Storage Space

Once the product has heaved it can remain in the same space and temperature for about three weeks. If this is more than enough time to consume it all, there is no need for alternative storage. Date each batch and/or check the pH occasionally for viability. With experience the home fermenter will learn how much to make for each batch and whether it will be necessary to consider additional storage methods for either the short or the long term.

Cooler temperatures slow down the fermentation process and extend shelf life; therefore, if longer term storage is required, the best location would be a cold storage area in a cellar or underground area or a refrigerator. The ferment should not be frozen as the consistency and flavor become far less desirable.

With proper storage, the ferments should last many months. Mature product will possess different qualities—the flavors deepen, the texture softens a little, the aroma is more subdued—and a new taste experience occurs from the exact same batch. As fresh, raw fermented cabbage becomes to the home fermenter as subtle an art as wine making, mature flavors and variations may bring about a whole new realm of culinary possibilities.

The Garden

There is no better place to find high-quality produce than a home garden. Having a piece of land on which to grow things is the ideal; however, most people can still grow things even if they live in a city apartment.

If blessed with a bit of land, consider growing cabbage and other favorite vegetables. Replace a manicured lawn with an herb garden. Plant berry bushes instead of decorative shrubs. Consider growing garlic and onions, tasteful additions to the cabbage mixture that are also prebiotics. Of course:

Consider growing everything organically, without the use of chemical pesticides, herbicides and fertilizers.

In doing so, a wonderful array of wildlife, including our all-important microorganisms, will be attracted and take up residence. This will in turn provide the gardener with plants with intact nutritional profiles for maximum health and flavor benefit.

The most important point to understand in growing anything in a garden is that variety is key. The industrial model of row-planting a single crop often fails without industrial, technological and/or chemical intervention—such as herbicides and genetic engineering—precisely because this is not how things grow naturally. We create these artificial systems that require artificial solutions. There becomes a doomed cycle of ever-increasing need for technology as weeds become more resistant and develop into "super-weeds," much as the superbugs discussed previously do. At some point, there may be no turning back as many crops could become dead ones, unable to adjust through natural selection.

Small, home gardens are ideal because by their nature they include a variety of plants and it is therefore easier to grow food organically. Important practices for healthy gardens include crop rotation to minimize pest and disease establishment, successive plantings to increase crop yield and

composting to enrich the soil. For "Northerners," cabbage can even be grown under cover and in the wintertime as it is a hardy crop.

Cabbage does have its enemies. The imported cabbageworm is the most prevalent and difficult problem, but there are plenty of simple, natural solutions available to eradicate them and other pests.

Help all vegetable crops stay safe from contamination by companion planting flowers, herbs and berries nearby, attracting beneficial insects, bees and birds. Introduce chickens or other fowl to the garden—they like to eat the juicy cabbageworm. There is also a natural product called Bt that works especially well on cabbageworms but does not harm other creatures. If the household contains children or grandchildren pay them a penny for each worm or moth they capture (children especially like to try batting the moths with a badminton racket).

If living in a city or in a suburban home with little land, growing food can still be accomplished. Growing fresh herbs is especially easy and saves a lot of money, but many vegetables, such as tomatoes and lettuce can be grown indoors, on a balcony or on a rooftop. In addition, some urban communities have dedicated space for cooperative gardens. There are many Internet sites on the subject that can be helpful. Of course, city dwellers can also grow beneficial microorganisms easily in small glass jars on a countertop—a bubbling treasure trove of probiotics and fresh vegetables with endless culinary possibilities.

The Market

Very few Americans are so self-sufficient in the new millennium that they do not have to shop for their food. We are truly so dependent on our industrial food and health systems that should a breakdown occur most of us would not have any idea what to do, other than hope that someone or something else comes to our rescue. In addition, most of us do not think about shopping as a political decision, but it most certainly is. As mentioned previously, it is perhaps the single most political action the average American can take, even over voting at the ballots. We need to think about where our money goes before we spend it, and then decide if we want it to go there.

Witness the surge in the organic foods market over the last decade or so. People want fewer chemicals in their food, and industry is responding partly because there is a lot of money to be made in the organics market right now, and partly (hopefully) because some of its leaders understand the importance of unnatural food to life and society.

Picture local farmers' markets or even supermarkets fully stocked with fresh, locally grown, tight-headed, plump, juicy cabbage year-round, instead of the sometimes pathetic wilted, dried-out heads found in many Northern supermarkets in wintertime. This could happen if demand went up—and it will, if people give this fermented foods lifestyle a chance.

When shopping for food in a supermarket, fresh food from the produce and meat departments are the wisest choices. Of course, within those departments higher or lesser quality will be available and decisions need to be made. In the produce department, rather than purchase a large bunch of fresh herbs when only a pinch is needed, consider growing your own in little hanging baskets by kitchen windows. Many produce departments now offer live herb plants for sale. In addition, learn which fruits and vegetables contain the highest concentration of chemicals and try to buy those organically grown.[11]

---

[11] Fortunately cabbage does not fall into the highest level category. Many fruits do, including especially apples, but there are now plenty of organic apples available in most produce departments. (By the way, fruits are not used in our

In the meat department, buying organic meats is preferable because certification regulates a variety of issues, such as what the animals are fed and what pharmaceuticals and/or chemicals are used during their lives or after. However, these products are hard to find in many supermarkets. In lieu of an organic label, look for animals fed their natural diets such as grass-fed beef and coming from farms as close to home as possible. Seek out a local farm and work with them on providing a share of their animals. Find cooperatives to join that may offer local and/or organic meats.

Meats in the deli department or the hot dog and bacon sections are best avoided. Try living without them or making sandwich meat at home from fresh meats and/or seek out organic franks and bacon.

Regarding seafood, try not to buy anything farm raised. Salmon is a widely farmed fish, and the first animal on a GMO track for human consumption. Contamination of wild salmon by GM salmon is a strong possibility as containment is virtually impossible. Of course, in the new millennium, most seafood is contaminated with mercury and other chemicals anyway, so pick and choose carefully. Avoid large, long-lived fish and bottom feeders.

From fresh produce and meats we move on in our supermarket experience to all those shiny, slick-packaging middle aisles. Much of what is contained within these aisles can be avoided. Yes, even those boxes and bags with the USDA

ferments). Some vegetables that are wonderful in cabbage ferments but contain high levels of chemicals include celery and sweet and hot peppers. These should be bought organically grown. Every year the Environmental Working Group (EWG) tests produce for dozens of different chemicals, so check the Internet for more information.

organic stamp of approval, and especially all those boxes and bags with the shameful use of the unregulated words "natural" or "all-natural." Do some research and much of the time these products will reveal their artificial nature in the form of GMOs and other undesirable substances.

Some middle-aisle products that are okay include certain coffees and teas, dried herbs and spices, vinegars and frozen whole fruits and vegetables; very few types of bread, pasta, oils and canned goods; and virtually no beverages, snack foods, salad dressings or mayonnaise.

Non-food items are often necessary, or at least they may seem to be. However, consider using cloth instead of paper items, food storage containers instead of disposable wraps and bags and non-antibacterial, low environmental impact detergents.

One middle-aisle of concern is the personal care aisle. Most makeup is unnecessary and applied to extremely sensitive areas of the body—the eyes, face and lips. Similarly, most soaps, shampoos, creams, hair dyes, perfumes, deodorants and bath products are loaded with chemicals, and these are quickly absorbed through the skin. These should be avoided, and later there will be suggestions on how to do this.

The last supermarket section most of us visit is the dairy aisle, and discussion here on these products would require an entire chapter. This is because of industrial processes that work against the nutritional value of the raw product, most significantly the germ-phobic regulation of pasteurization,[12] and the vehement institutional defense of it.

---

[12] Other processes, such as homogenization, irradiation and chemical additives are detrimental to dairy products as well.

A true fermented foods lifestyle would most certainly suggest dairy products be fermented or soured into yogurt, kefir, sour cream and cheeses, but it would absolutely require these be created from raw milk.

Virtually all commercial dairy products are pasteurized, with the rare exception of a few cheeses. This destroys many nutrients and renders nutrient absorption nearly impossible, including the most important one for which consuming dairy is recommended—calcium. What good is drinking gallons or eating pounds of something for a nutritional benefit when that nutrient cannot be absorbed by the body?

In addition, the high heat of pasteurization kills not only bad bacteria, it kills the good. Therefore, if living without dairy is not an option, find a local source for raw milk (and sour it at home) or find fermented raw milk products.[13] If necessary, purchase only those pasteurized dairy products that are soured, then try to find those with labels stating it contains live cultures and perhaps this can compensate for other pitfalls (but make sure to avoid the high-sugar and artificially flavored yogurts and kefirs).

One item usually found with dairy products is orange and other juices. Just totally avoid these—they are nothing but concentrated sugar and they are far from being fresh. Squeezed orange juice can sit in tanks for a year while waiting to be "re-flavored" using undisclosed ingredients created by

---

[13] If you can. Not easy due to very strict raw milk and food safety guidelines, which have little to do with safety and more to do with centralization of power over our food and water. If these are controlled, people are controlled— another illustration of the politics of food. Interesting that two very dangerous substances are found everywhere—alcohol and tobacco—but raw milk is almost invisible to the average consumer.

chemists from the flavor and fragrance industries. There is really nothing healthy about fruit juices and they are expensive and come in all that disposable, slick, landfill packaging; instead, just eat the fresh fruit. Or, try the wonderful array of orange herbal teas instead.

In sum:

Try to avoid purchasing foods containing chemicals, GMOs, nanotech particles or any other laboratory or factory created product.

Also avoid purchasing foods that have undergone denaturing food processes such as irradiation, pasteurization and homogenization.

A portion of household foods should be made up of fresh, raw fermented forms where possible.

3 *The What*

Cabbage

As previously discussed, cabbage should be as fresh as possible for the best possible ferments. Growing it in a home garden is ideal; however, if this is not possible, buy it from as local a source as possible. For the first time fermenter, the plain green variety of cabbage is recommended. Other varieties, such as red, Savoy and Napa cabbages can be tried as fermenting experience is gained.

The best green cabbage is tight-headed and heavy. Peel back the dark outer leaves and take a look at the next layers. The inner leaves should be shiny, plump and juicy looking. For home processing, buy smaller heads as they are easier to cut and handle.

This book recommends processing cabbage in batches of five pounds, about two medium-sized heads. This will produce about three quarts of ferment, depending on the type and amount of other vegetables and herbs used.

Sea Salt

For any use at all, but especially for fermenting cabbage:

Use only finely ground natural salts, not processed table salt.

There is little sense in taking the time to produce as fresh and as chemically free a product as possible and then taint it with processed table salt. In fact, do away with commercially produced and processed table salt altogether;[14] however, do not do away with natural salts despite the outdated and incorrect medical advice that abounds.

All salts are not equal. Do the research and learn about the difference between processed table salt and natural salts such as unprocessed Himalayan and Hawaiian Alaea salts. Processed salt is chemically treated and heated to very high temperatures. This processing changes the composition and health benefits of pure salt. Yes, natural salts are perfectly fine and in fact needed substances in the human diet, despite what doctors might say, and they are essential in producing raw, fresh fermented cabbage. In addition, most commercial salts also contain dextrose. Yes, that popular GMO corn additive.

Fortunately, unrefined sea salt can be found in virtually any store now. Purchase fine-ground sea salt (and make sure it is unprocessed with no additives) for consistency in the ferment recipes to start; however, experiment with other exotic natural salts, such as finely ground Himalayan, as experience with fermentation grows. These and other salts are

---

[14] Including products that contain it. Buy salt-free versions of everything, then add sea salt later.

not only beneficial to human health in their natural state but contain valuable trace minerals as well.

Vegetables

Certain vegetables in addition to cabbage should be grown or purchased and added to the chopped cabbage if different flavors are desired. Garlic, onions, ginger, fresh and dried herbs and spices should be on hand at all times. These are items that keep well, contain a lot of flavor and can be added to the mixture quickly and easily if out of other fresh vegetables.

Do not use anything other than fresh vegetables to add to the mixture.

No canned or frozen vegetables should be used, with a few exceptions such as small amounts of ripe olives and pickled jalapeno peppers. These can be rinsed and used to add some nice flavor to several of the recipes.

Fresh onions provide a lot of flavor and any variety can be used. The Cabbage Cove uses sweet yellow, red, scallions, shallots and leeks among others, but any other in the onion family can be used. Fresh garlic and fresh ginger provide even more flavor and work very well in the ferments. Remember, the best flavor is attained by using fresh onions, garlic and ginger. Take the time to peel and chop—it is worth the effort.

In addition to the aforementioned vegetables, favorite fresh vegetables the Cabbage Cove uses in its recipes include organic celery, organic sweet peppers, organic hot peppers, radish, horseradish, daikon, green beans, spinach, beets, lemongrass and carrots; however, certainly the home fermenter is not limited to these. Experiment with favorites in small batches, add the appropriate seasonings and create your own recipes. There is space in this book to take notes and write down favorite combinations.

Herbs

Any fresh or dried herbs can be used to flavor the cabbage; however, fresh are preferred, primarily because the flavor is superior, but also because fresh herbs will not absorb precious moisture as using too much dried can. As previously mentioned, growing herbs in the home kitchen or garden is far less expensive than store bought and very easy to do.

Fresh cilantro, oregano, parsley, sage, rosemary, thyme, basil, dill, marjoram, stevia, mint...these are only a few of the varieties used in the recipes. Experiment, mix and match and use favorites to see what works best. Herbs can be chopped finely, coarsely or used whole-leaf in any of the recipes, and will be far easier to chop if dry and unwashed. Simply brush or shake off any dirt or other particles, and do not worry so much about "germs."

Another wonderful addition to the chopped cabbage is seeds. There are three in particular the Cabbage Cove keeps at hand always: caraway, sesame and coriander; however, any seeds may be used whether whole or ground. Seeds can add a tremendous amount of flavor to the ferments.

Spices

Most of the recipes also use many different dried spices, but as with dried herbs, care must be taken not to overuse anything dried for fear of robbing the mixture of too much moisture. Dried spices, which are usually finer in texture, tend to do this more than dried herbs, which are usually leafier and coarser.

Many spices are staples in the Cabbage Cove kitchen, such as red pepper flakes, cayenne pepper, black pepper, cumin, curry, cinnamon, cardamom and apple pie and pumpkin pie spices. Sometimes even a little hot sauce can be added as well. These make wonderful additions to the recipes and in some cases make all the difference in attaining the desired flavor and effect.

As with vegetables:

Try to grow or buy organic herbs, seeds and spices in order to avoid chemicals and damaging commercial processes such as irradiation.

Water

The main use for water in the Cabbage Cove kitchen is as a brine to add when packing the cabbage mixture into the jars. Try to use only pure water devoid of chemicals. Home filtration is preferred to buying water if tap water is tainted.

Verboten

Never add any animal products to the mixture. This includes all meats, fish, dairy and animal fats such as butter. A little oil for flavor is okay; for example, sesame or walnut oil, but only use a small amount. This book deals only with cabbage and vegetable fermentation, and foods other than these will produce mixed results or fail altogether and be dangerous to eat.

Avoid adding fruits as well. The only exception to the fruit rule are those that are high-acid, such as tomatoes and citrus fruits. Fresh squeezed lemon or lime juice is especially delicious.

It is important not to add any additional salt to the mixture. First, salt added to extract moisture from the cabbage is measured very precisely in order to create a balance that will destroy the harmful bacteria yet keep the beneficial ones thriving. Salted water, or brine, is added to help shore up the moisture content while maintaining the same levels of salt. Not only would adding more salt change the balance and perhaps kill the good bacteria, it is wasteful.

Use common sense and avoid doing anything at first that deviates too much from the processes suggested in this book. It is important to have simple successes and enjoy eating raw, fresh fermented cabbage before any major failures in processing occur and possibly interfere with establishing a new, probiotic lifestyle.

4 The How

Preparing

Begin with clean, not chemically sterile, surfaces, and bring out all the necessary preparation equipment. To recapitulate, equipment includes a food processor or sharp chef's knife for chopping the cabbage, smaller knives or other utensils for chopping additional vegetables and herbs, cutting board, mixing bowls, scale, measuring spoons and cups, glass jars, lids and bands and any preferred spoons or scrapers.

First prepare the brine, as it takes a little time for the sea salt to dissolve in the water. In a two- or four-cup glass container, add two or four cups of filtered, purified room temperature water or clean tap or well water along with 1.5 or 3 tablespoons of sea salt respectively. Stir well. While preparing cabbage mixture, continue to stir occasionally. Brine may also be prepared in advance and stored covered in a glass container.

Prepare cabbage and other vegetables and herbs. Cut cabbage in quarters and remove toughest part of core. Cut away any severely blemished, discolored or spoiled pieces if they exist.

Weigh all quarters first by placing a large bowl on the scale and setting the scale to 0, adding the cabbage and then noting the weight. Finely chop the cabbage in food processor or with large knife. If using a food processor, try the pulse setting a few times. This will help chop evenly with minimal processing. Place all of the chopped cabbage in large bowl.

Now the cabbage must be salted. To meet the 2.5% salt ideal for highest quality ferments (between 2 and 3.5 is acceptable), 0.6, or a little more than ½ tablespoon, of sea salt should be used for each pound (16 ounces) of cabbage (0.0375 per ounce). Two pounds of cabbage would require 1.2 tablespoons, three would require 1.8, four 2.4 and five would require 3 tablespoons of fine ground sea salt.

Sprinkle sea salt evenly throughout the chopped cabbage, mixing in well. If batch weight is more than a few pounds, sprinkle a little, mix and repeat several times. At this point the mixture should "rest" for at least 10 minutes to allow time for the salt to draw out the moisture from the cabbage. The mixture should start to glisten and water will start to collect at the bottom of the bowl. In the meantime, the other vegetables and herbs can be prepared. Of course, it is not necessary to add any other ingredients if a plain variety is desired. Simply skip to the packing stage.

Dice or chop the vegetables into fairly small uniform pieces for even distribution in the mixture. Garlic, onions and ginger should be peeled and finely chopped. Herbs should be chopped finely although a few large leaves may be added for visual effect as well as flavor. Remember, any major blemishes, discolorations or spoiled sections of any vegetables or herbs should be removed and placed into the compost heap, fed to animals or discarded. Do not use them for the ferments.

Mix all ingredients together with the cabbage thoroughly. If any spices are to be added, sprinkle just a little evenly on top, mix and taste. Add more if necessary. Once the flavor is acceptable, the mixture may be packed into the glass jars.

Following are some of the ingredients for several of the Cabbage Cove's most popular varieties. These are suggested only; fermenters can feel free to omit and add and experiment in developing their craft. Remember not to overload the cabbage mixture with other ingredients—cabbage needs to remain the main ingredient—and all garlic, ginger and herbs are, of course, better when fresh.

Cinnamon: fresh stevia leaf or 100% natural stevia powder, cinnamon, real vanilla extract. Optional: apple pie spice or pumpkin pie spice instead of cinnamon.

German: yellow onion, caraway seed.

Greek: organic green pepper, yellow onion, green beans, rinsed sliced or chopped ripe black pitted olives, garlic, mint, dill, oregano, bay leaf.

Indian: organic chili peppers, ginger, onion, garlic, cilantro, curry powder, cumin, turmeric, mustard seed, coriander, cinnamon, cardamom, or any desirable combination of these.

Italian: garlic, yellow onion, plum tomatoes, oregano, basil, sage, Italian seasoning.

Korean: radish, scallions, garlic, ginger, crushed red pepper flakes.

Mexican: tomatoes, scallions and/or yellow onion, cilantro, rinsed sliced ripe black pitted olives, rinsed diced pickled jalapeno peppers or fresh jalapeno or habanero peppers (preferably organic), cumin. Optional: few dashes Tabasco or other favorite hot sauce.

Spicy: organic chili or any other very hot peppers, garlic, crushed red pepper flakes, cayenne pepper, hot sauce.[15]

Thai: organic hot chili peppers, shallots, ginger, fresh cilantro, fresh mint, fresh squeezed lemon and/or lime juice, ground black pepper, lemongrass.

Ukrainian: beets, carrots, onion, garlic, fresh dill.

Packing

Fill a pint or quart glass Mason jar with the mixture and pack product down using a plastic or wooden utensil. A small-to medium-sized hand works too if using wide-mouth jars. The product should be moist enough that when packing the juices rise to the top. Release air bubbles with a plastic tool by inserting it all the way to the bottom in a few places. Keep packing and releasing air bubbles until the product reaches the "shoulder"[16] of the jar.

---

[15] Varieties that taste extremely hot and spicy prior to fermentation will taste less so after; however, the unique and subtle nuances of the ingredients are boosted. In other words, less burn, more flavor. This is especially true of horseradish, which tends to lose most of its burn but delivers amazing horseradish flavor. Remember, the fresher the ingredient the more potent it will be.

[16] Just where the glass begins to curve toward the neck, or threaded area. The

Now top off with the brine, bringing the liquid to the bottom of the neck, or threads, of the jar. Place the lid on top and screw on the band securely, but not too tightly. If there is a little left over, wrap and place in refrigerator for use in cooking, or add a little homemade mayonnaise for instant Cole slaw. Store the jars in the chosen fermentation space.

Neck
Brine level
Shoulder

Product level

Fermenting

Each day check the product by unscrewing the band a little to release any gases (burping), without disturbing the lid. If the product is kept at a temperature in the ideal range (65-72 degrees F), it should heave after a few days. Be prepared for bubbling over and the release of gases.

Remember to protect the areas and surfaces underneath the jars as liquid may seep out and over. If heaving is suspected as imminent (jar band becomes harder to unscrew due to liquid seepage onto the threads or the lid is puckered or puffed out), burping can be done in a sink.

---

shoulder and neck are apparent with the quart-sized Mason jars. If using pint sizes however, the wide-mouth jar does not have a shoulder. Therefore, fill the product to about an inch and a half below the threads.

Be prepared! Sometimes heaving is so intense, it pushes a fair amount up over the top of the jar. Have a spoon and container ready to scoop extra for immediate use. Dry the band, outside of jar, outside threads and top of lid if moist and reseal the jar. Now, taste the product. This should be the most pleasurable experience in the entire process as the texture and flavors are at their peak. The product is bubbly, crunchy and bursting with life. However, a variety of microorganisms still need time to develop, so try not to eat all ferments up at once all the time, but rather develop a strategy for rotation and use at different stages of fermentation.

At the ideal temperature range fermentation should continue for about three weeks, but if most of the product has not been used by about two weeks, set the jars in cool storage in order to extend its life. If fermenting at cooler temperatures, the processing time will be longer but so will the shelf life. Under the right conditions, ferments can last for many, many months.

After heaving, it is not necessary to burp the jars every day, but check the product occasionally for color, taste and moisture. As the ferment is used, push down the remaining product to keep it moist in its own juices. Top off with a little premade brine if necessary. If there is any discoloration in the top layer, remove and discard it. If desired, check the acidity of the product using pH paper with a range of 0-6. Remember, viable ferments usually maintain a pH below 4.5. This is the level at which food will spoil if not refrigerated, because it is the level at which harmful microorganisms can begin to thrive. Most successful ferments will maintain a pH at or below 3.9, and over time may reach a pH much lower, even to 2.5 or so.

Therefore, as a general rule, if a pH climbs to around 4.0 over time, refrigerate and use as soon as possible just as you would produce purchased in a supermarket.

Using

Ferments that are kept in the ideal range for short periods are wonderful because they do not need warming in recipes. They are at the perfect temperature to start. However, they will not last as long as those placed in cool storage or refrigeration right after heaving occurs. Usually a combination of both strategies is ideal. With experience, fermenters will determine what works best for them.

Remember however that if the product is cold; cooking it will result in the destruction of microorganisms. Therefore, warm only very gently. The easiest way to do this is to add it to warm food, that is, unless the food has been microwaved. The Cabbage Cove does not recommend using a microwave under any circumstances. Period. More on this later in the chapter on "Unsolicited Advice," but for those who simply cannot live without a microwave, do not cook the ferments in the microwave nor mix it in to microwaved food. In time and with experience, fermenters may come to learn that their creations are all the fast food they need, and hopefully will do away with these terribly harmful appliances.

Ideally, the fermented cabbage is eaten in small amounts, fresh and raw, with every meal and as a snack in between. The product as described herein is concentrated, both in nutrition and flavor, so a little goes a long way. Once the multitude of ways in which it can be used is discovered, making this wonderful, healthy, fresh food a regular part of the diet is extremely simple.

5 The Recipes

Breakfast

Perhaps more than any other meal, breakfast is one for which people have very definite ideas of what they want to eat. Most certainly the majority of Americans would not consider fermented cabbage one of those foods.

Food industry and its medical and governmental cronies have drummed into our heads that breakfast is the most important meal of the day, but this is just not so—especially if that meal does us more harm than good. That is precisely what the cereal, bread, muffin, toaster tart, microwave breakfast sandwich, fill-in-the-blank high sugar, high chemical American breakfast does. Especially disheartening is the number of ways in which GMO grains loaded with sugar and chemicals are packaged as acceptable and even nutritious enough for consumption by U.S. children.

Far better traditional breakfast foods would be those protein and fruit choices, such as eggs and berries, but make sure the meat choices are organic, local or not highly processed or loaded with nitrates and nitrites. Coffee and tea are fine beverages, but fruit juices, especially orange juice, are bad choices.

If people think about fresh fermented cabbage simply as a chopped vegetable, possible uses become more apparent for any meal. However, it is possible to use the cinnamon fermented cabbage a substitute for cereal as well. Try these recipes and then create your own.

Cabbage "Oatmeal": place a small amount of cinnamon variety in a bowl; add diced fruit, berries, nuts and/or sweetener of choice.[17] Cream or whipped cream may be added if desired. The consistency is that of oatmeal and it is delicious. Apples, raisins and walnuts work particularly well. This is an excellent probiotic rich, low carb[18] replacement for cereal.

Cabbage Cove Omelet: Melt coconut oil in a small pan on low heat while beating two eggs. Pour eggs into pan and let set, then flip to briefly cook other side. Cheese may be added just to melt. Remove from heat and place about ¼ cup of any

---

[17] To keep calories and carbs down, add stevia, xylitol or other no-calorie, natural sweetener. Avoid artificial sweeteners such as sucralose, saccharin and aspartame like the plague. The best choice and gaining in popularity is an herb called "stevia." About 30 times sweeter than cane sugar, a little goes a long way. However, beware, as food conglomerates are jumping on the stevia bandwagon and pushing out smaller manufacturers on supermarket shelves. The trouble with this is that the larger concerns are, as usual, cutting into the stevia food industry GMOs and other chemicals that are totally unnecessary and harmful. Make sure the stevia used is homegrown leaf, or read the labels on store-bought products and avoid those with harmful additives. The best stevia products on the market contain organic stevia extract and inulin fiber (a prebiotic). If other sweeteners are deemed necessary, stick to natural raw honey (except for infants), maple syrup or organic cane sugar if absolutely necessary.

[18] Depending upon the sweetener used.

variety onto eggs and spread around evenly. Fold ½ over to make omelet shape. Serve with berries, organic bacon or sweet potato hash browns. Alternatively, add chopped precooked meats such as bacon or ham and additional vegetables such as onions, peppers, and mushrooms to the pan and sauté lightly before adding eggs. There is usually no need to season as the ferments provide plenty of saltiness and other flavors.

Cabbage Cove Scrambled Eggs: Similar to the omelet except the eggs are stirred constantly instead of leaving to cook flat.

Cabbage Cove Breakfast Sandwich: Line whole grain flatbread or sprouted grain tortilla with bacon or ham, scrambled eggs and a favorite fresh fermented cabbage variety. Drizzle or spray a little coconut oil evenly, roll up half way, fold in edges and finish rolling for a delicious and energizing breakfast on the go.

Eggs Benedict a la Cove: Make regular eggs Benedict with English muffin, Canadian bacon, poached eggs and Hollandaise sauce, or substitute toasted sourdough bread, fried green tomatoes or cooked sweet potato slices for the English muffin. After all is assembled, sprinkle the Lemon Pepper or favorite variety on top. Similarly, for any dish calling for Hollandaise or Béarnaise sauce, mix in some Lemon-Pepper variety for a new take on any dish.

Quick Breakfast: Toast one or two slices of sourdough or favorite hearty whole grain bread. Spread on organic coconut oil instead of butter. There are coconut and other oil sprays available in most markets now too. Top with cinnamon or any variety of fresh fermented cabbage and spread over toast evenly.

Lunch

It is truly better to eat only when hungry, but the three-meal-a-day idea is so ingrained and the sandwich such a part of our culture that some lunch ideas are presented here. Once probiotics take hold and vitality is increased, a natural routine may take over and people may discover it is better to eat one brunch and a snack rather than two separate filling meals. The secret is to listen to the body.

In addition, many people rush through daytime meals; it is almost always better to relax and eat more slowly. Try making the time for one relaxing daytime meal from either the breakfast or lunch ideas here, and if hungry before supper try some of the snack ideas below.

Chicken Salad Sandwich: Dice a small serving of precooked chicken breast into bite sized pieces. Mix with equal amounts of any variety, then add a little homemade or organic mayonnaise to taste.[19] Serve in Romaine lettuce leaves, on top of chopped lettuce or on toasted sourdough or other whole grain bread.

Tuna Salad Sandwich: Same preparation as chicken salad only using canned tuna instead of diced chicken.

Egg Salad Sandwich: Same preparation as chicken salad only using chopped hard boiled eggs instead of diced chicken.

---

[19] Avoid commercial mayonnaise—its main ingredient is usually GMO soybean oil.

Fast Green Salad: Chop lettuce and place in bowl. Mix in any variety to create a healthy, probiotic-rich, super-fast salad—the dicing and chopping of the salad ingredients is already done. Salad dressing[20] is not needed as the ferments are delicious and moist enough. If desired for a more filling salad add a little shredded cheese and/or nuts.

Perfect Probiotic Pitas: Stuff a warmed pita pocket with a mixture of the Greek variety, feta cheese, fresh homegrown sprouts and some chopped lettuce if desired. Drizzle with extra virgin olive oil and enjoy.

Cabbage Cove Roll Up: Simply line a Romaine lettuce leaf with any variety for a fast and easy sandwich. Get creative by adding cheese strips, tomatoes, sandwich meat, onion, sprouts, the previous night's leftovers and/or the Cabbage Cove's favorite, thinly sliced avocado.

Supper

Supper is a time for all household members to gather together and share their thoughts and experiences of the day with each other as well as a great, home-cooked meal. Or is it? Far too many families rush through this meal and miss the opportunity to not only bond with children or other loved ones, but to greatly improve their digestion and the bioavailability of nutrients. Think about what draws everyone away from the dinner table, and decide if it is more important than the time together for bonding and good health.

---

[20] As with commercial mayo, avoid commercial salad dressings, which are loaded with GMO oils, bad salt, sugars, chemicals and preservatives. It is very easy to make homemade dressings with better ingredients, such as extra virgin olive oil, vinegars, homemade mayo, lemon juice, spices and herbs.

Create an atmosphere conducive to good digestion and calm conversation. Low or natural lighting, soft music or wind chimes, pretty tableware, no television and no phone interruptions can make a huge difference in promoting good digestion, and therefore increasing the absorption of nutrients. Yes, mealtime atmosphere is that important.

Absolutely no use of cell phones at the table should be allowed, and this applies to adults as well as to children. Nor should disagreements become heated at the dinner table—if there is an argument brewing, save it for later discussion. There may be resistance to these ideas initially if they are not already part of the household norm, but in time all but the most technologically addicted people will unwittingly realize the benefits and enjoy.

Following are suggestions for many types of supper meals and foods; however, virtually any favorite meal can be adapted to incorporate fresh fermented cabbage with vast arrays of flavors, even if nothing more than a small bowl of complimentarily flavored ferment is placed on the table or plate as a condiment.

Meats: Use any fresh uncooked variety as traditional sauerkraut would be used on hot dogs, hamburgers (see recipes below), veal, chicken, sausage, bison, turkey...any meat can be enhanced with fermented cabbage. Try different varieties with different meats for unique and flavorful combinations. Try a lemony variety with fish, a peppery variety with chicken or turkey and a spicy variety with beef. But do not limit your imagination; sometimes the strangest sounding combinations turn out to be wonderful.

Cabbage Cove Pizza: Toast a slice or two of sourdough or favorite hearty whole grain bread. Slice on the diagonal to form pizza slice shape (sort of). Top each triangle with a spray of coconut oil and mozzarella cheese and melt gently under broiler or toaster oven, being careful not to burn top of cheese. Spoon on the Italian variety and press into melted cheese. Children especially love this flavor. Be creative and mix and match different cheeses with different varieties. Make international pizzas by matching a variety to its complimentary cheese; for example, layer Swiss cheese with the German variety or feta cheese with the Greek. Cabbage Cove Pizzas work well for breakfast, lunch, snack or supper.

Dylan's Blazin' Chili Dog: Spread sour cream on the inside of a potato hot dog bun and follow with a layer of homemade chili, a layer of the Spicy variety, the hot dog and favorite hot sauce.

Cabbage Stuffed Potato or Sweet Potato: Bake potatoes or sweet potatoes in oven until a fork pierces them easily. Scoop out insides and put into mixing bowl, leaving shells intact. Add fermented cabbage choice, drizzle with a little extra virgin olive oil, and if desired a little butter and/or sour cream, chopped scallions, bacon bits, or any diced vegetable or leftovers of choice. Mix together and put back into skin shell. Top with cheese if desired and place back in oven until cheese melts, or simply serve immediately if temperature is good and additional ingredients did not cool the potato down too much. Experiment with different mixtures for new taste experiences.

Hot Dogs and Hamburgers: Use any fresh fermented cabbage variety as sauerkraut would be used on hot dogs and hamburgers. Try putting a hot dog in a Romaine lettuce leaf to avoid using a high-carb bun, and top with a different ferment each time to avoid boredom with ordinary franks. The Indian is especially delicious and reminiscent of mustard, relish and sauerkraut all in one. Try organic, chicken or turkey franks too. Serve beef, bison, chicken, turkey or veggie burgers slow cooked in coconut oil on top of a bed of lettuce. Add any variety that has been slightly warmed in the cooled down pan juices on top. Add cheese on top of burger if desired.[21] Good for any meal and hot dogs are especially fast—just find a good one without chemicals and from a trusted meat source.

Cove Curried Chicken: Place any boneless chicken, preferably dark meat, into crock-pot or slow cooker and just cover with chicken stock and/or filtered water. Follow appliance directions for length of time and temperature to cook through. When chicken is ready, add sliced yellow onions to crock-pot just to heat and soften a little. Serve mixture including a little liquid over rice on plate and add generous helping of the Indian variety spread a little over the top. Place ½ diced or sliced avocado and fresh cilantro sprigs on top. The Thai variety is also delicious prepared this way.

Christina's Awesome Burger: Cook burger or cheeseburger of choice and place on a bed of cooked organic chopped spinach. Put on a scoop of Mexican, Spicy or favorite variety fresh fermented cabbage and top with diced or sliced

---

[21] Again, there is no need to add any condiment to hot dogs and hamburgers made in this fashion. Avoid commercial ketchup with its GMO corn syrup and bad salt, and commercial mustard with its bad salt and variety of GMO and chemical additives, such as citric acid and artificial colors. Note that some giant manufacturers are finally starting to offer organic versions of their products.

avocado. Serve with a spoonful of salsa and/or sour cream and tortilla chips or sweet potato fries on the side.

Cabbagery Beef: Sauté ground beef on low heat in pan with coconut oil and chop and stir until browned through. Add a little sea salt and diced onion, and cook onion until just soft. Remove from heat and let cool a little. Using a slotted spoon, serve mixture on a bed of rice, cooked greens or bed of lettuce leaving juices behind. Mix any variety fresh fermented cabbage into cooled pan juices and serve over beef and rice pouring juices on top as well.   Top with diced avocado, grated parmesan cheese and/or diced tomatoes. Serve with hot sauce if desired.

Luke's Mexican Mac n Cheese: Quick and easy...make favorite macaroni and cheese recipe. Before serving, mix in the Mexican variety. Try Italian, Spicy or Greek Mac n Cheese too.

Snacks, Apps & Etc.

Mini Cabbage Cove Pizzas: Follow recipe for Cabbage Cove pizzas above, but instead of slices of toast try using favorite cracker. Just warm a tray of crackers and cheese gently in oven or toaster oven then press into cheese a dollop of any fresh variety.

Sue's Scrumptious Scoops: Place small pieces of cheese in tortilla "scoops" and top with favorite variety, placing desired number of scoops on oven tray. Warm gently in low oven or toaster oven just to melt cheese. Serve and observe the oohs and ahs.

Guacabbole: Mash avocado with a little lemon or lime juice, then mix in any variety. Use anywhere guacamole is used—on top of salads, beside meats, with enchiladas, in black bean soup or served with tortilla chips. Or, just eat with a spoon.

Cabbage Cove Nachos: Prepare tortilla, pita or any other sturdy chips on oven tray, topping with grated cheese of choice followed by a layer of diced vegetables such as green onions, olives, peppers and/or tomatoes, followed by another layer of grated cheese. Place in low oven just to melt cheese. Remove and sprinkle with fresh ferment of choice. Serve with salsa, guacamole or guacabbole and/or sour cream. For fast C.C. nachos, omit the layer of diced vegetables.

Lynn's Compañero de Margarita: Place whole tortilla chips on a plate or tray. Add a dollop of Mexican variety and top with a chunk or slice of avocado. A dollop of premade guacamole works as well. A fast and delicious app.

Probiotic Salsa: Simply replace salsa with any favorite variety for use anywhere salsa would be used, especially with tortilla chips for a fast and delicious snack. Or mix any variety into a con queso sauce for dipping or pouring over meats or pasta.

Cove Slaw: Mix a little homemade or organic mayonnaise with any fresh fermented cabbage variety for the best probiotic-rich, instant Cole slaw. Or, omit mayonnaise and serve any variety at picnics instead of Cole slaw—it will not spoil as mayonnaise laden food will, lasting all day long and retaining its wonderful flavor.

On the Go: Many people have reported simply bringing a little fermented cabbage and a spoon with them wherever they go. It is easy to do and no cooler is required. Grab a few crackers or chips too if desired. Filling yet energizing.

Richard's "Only Half Guilty" Dessert: Mix vanilla ice cream with an equal mixture of cinnamon variety. Hard to believe, but this is delicious. The cabbage is crunchy and reminiscent of walnuts. If desired, walnuts and raisins can be added too.

Although cooking destroys valuable probiotics, it is not necessary to always limit the ferments to raw use only.

Certainly make room in the diet for a good amount of raw consumption, but experiment with different of ways of cooking with the ferments as well. There are still positive time-saving, flavor and digestibility qualities even if probiotics are lost in the cooking process. As long as enough raw ferment is eaten there is nothing wrong with cooking a little of it too.

6 *Your Recipes*

7 *The Unsolicited Advice*

There are a few bits of advice (unsolicited) that are important to note as they may help enhance a probiotic lifestyle. Hopefully, they may help stimulate some thought on areas of life needing change on a broader scale. Some of these points have already been discussed previously; however, it is important to underscore a few of the vital ones here.

On Toxic Lifestyle

There is little that is of more immediate and long-term concern to human life than the overwhelming amount of chemicals, laboratory altered substances and radiation that bombards us all on a daily basis. Very few media outlets discuss this to the degree they discuss the sometimes absurd activities of celebrities or sports figures and the latest viral video. Therefore, it is important to educate ourselves rather than rely on frivolous media outlets for information.

Where choices exist, choose wisely. Try to minimize exposure to chemicals, GMOs, nanotechnology and radiation wherever possible and vote with ballots and dollars to help promote changing some of society's harmful practices.

Currently, industry has been waging war on both GMO labeling laws and USDA Organic standards that currently forbid GMOs. Fortunately, organic standards have held up against industry pressure. Labeling laws are slowly being introduced in various states across the U.S. So there is still hope people can know to a degree what is in some food and household products. In any case, it is just good practice to:

Read labels before buying anything and avoid products that contain lab-created or -altered ingredients.

Pharmaceuticals are included on the avoidance list if at all possible. Regardless of condition, most doctors suggest changing diet or exercising more. This is good advice that perhaps could be tried before taking drugs. Drugs can work against the healthiest lifestyle, most commonly in the form of weight gain, but sometimes with very serious side effects. There are certainly many drugs that are valuable and lifesaving, but far too many are over-prescribed and overused, for example this work's nemesis, antibiotics.

Another dangerous technological byproduct often ignored en masse is radiation. Think about how certain appliances are used, such as microwave ovens and cell phones. Microwave ovens are simply unnecessary, but feel too convenient for many people to consider doing without. If it has to be in the home, do several things. First, never microwave in plastic. Chemicals in plastic leach into food. Second, place it away from the main area in a corner somewhere—especially place it away from little faces. Radiation in all its forms is especially damaging to children. Later, when they marry and want to have children and cannot, no one searches deeply for the reasons why. All that is left is emotional suffering.

In fact, it seems most people have no idea that their new best friends, cell phones, emit dangerous radiation. Always use the speaker phone, Bluetooth or headsets, and:

Never hold a cell phone to your head and try to keep it away from other parts of your body as much as possible.

Especially, never put it next to your head at night. Do not assume it is safer when off either—it still omits radiation. Try reducing its use, especially in areas of weak reception, and switch to a landline where possible. Other sources of radiation include WiFi, cell towers and medical and dental X-rays. This bombardment can cause a host of molecular changes resulting in diseases such as cancer and infertility, and who knows what else for the future of the human race.

All of these types of exposure are hard to monitor and all the more reason to make probiotics a staple in the diet. With the unprecedented toxic exposure of the new millennium, our tiny friends along with our cells are subject to damage and death, leaving us unprotected from additional onslaught from viral and bacterial infection.

Also remember that much research done in the new millennium is industry-driven so it is important to do self-research or seek out those who have in order to compare recommendations and make informed decisions. If this is done, in time it will become difficult to trust mass media outlets for much more than sales pitches.

On Healthcare

We receive much advice from popular talk shows and advertising on how to make personal healthcare decisions, but these sources are not always reliable. It is important to talk directly with doctors instead of believing everything seen on television or the Internet, but it is also important to become involved personally. When seeking a practitioner, look for those who are interested in working with patients as healthcare partners, not those who are only interested in human herd obedience. Respect goes both way in personal healthcare decisions. The patient is the one with the most to lose, so it is important to never feel intimidated by health care providers. Have them explain everything and answer all questions. If a feeling of intimidation encroaches, take the reins and switch doctors.

Without the good bacteria in our guts working to keep our immune system operating properly, we become far more susceptible to illness and disease, yet modern medicine does not adopt as one of its main tenets helping people to learn about making, choosing and eating probiotic-rich foods.

Some doctors will advise people eat yogurt, but as discussed previously, most yogurt is damaged by pasteurization and does not contain live cultures. Some doctors may even recommend a probiotic supplement—which is a better source than none—but supplements just do not have the whole food benefit of certain enzymes and other natural interactions, many of which we may not yet fully understand. Further, these recommendations are primarily in reaction to antibiotic use rather than preventative and many still do not recommend them at all. In fact, many practitioners neglect to limit antibiotic use despite urgings to do so from their own American Medical Association.

It is up to us to learn about the great importance of pro- and pre-biotics to our health rather than rely solely on modern medicine for accurate information.

Antibiotics have been so routinely prescribed and are so commonplace that most people do not understand just how dangerous they are. Think carefully before taking them, because the entire body will be affected. If unavoidable, load up on probiotic supplements and foods for the duration and for some time after. Once the illness has past, make pro- and pre-biotics a regular part of the diet. Also, avoid antibacterial soaps, hand cleansers and cleaning products too.

There are three essential factors for health needing mention here; they are water, rest and light. Recommendations change all the time as to how much water and sleep a body needs. The key is to not listen to recommendations—listen to the body instead. When tired, rest or sleep. When thirsty, drink pure water. Period.

Of course, water is essential to life. However, some sources claim as much as 90 percent of Earth's water is contaminated. In the new millennium, water filtration at least is essential.

Drink pure, unadulterated water when thirsty.

Another concern of the future may very well be water availability, so think about from where water will come if a current main source becomes unavailable.

Rest and sleep are also essential. Our bodies need to rejuvenate and repair. If sleepy during the day, take a 15 minute nap. When tired in the evening, go to sleep.

Sleep when tired in a dark, quiet room.

Whenever resting or sleeping, darken the room totally and keep it quiet. Especially, do not keep a television in the bedroom or keep the television off; it will interrupt deep sleep. Soft music is okay if it shuts off after a while. Also, do not drink too much before bed or sleep will be interrupted for a bathroom break.

If waking in the middle of the night, go right back to bed in the dark, quiet room and think lovely thoughts rather than turn on a T.V. or grab a cell phone. Remember, do not keep the phone near the bed.

Natural light is mentioned here because it too is a nutrient of sorts, but one that most people do not recognize as important. Modern life is replete with artificial light and ever increasing amounts of projected versus reflected light. Attention span is severely affected—it is only about 30 seconds when reading or viewing with projected light versus 30 minutes or more with reflected light.

Expose the eyes to daylight on a regular basis and more natural lighting at nighttime, such as fire, candle, starlight or gaslight.

Purchase full spectrum bulbs for more natural lighting in the home. Read from printed paper instead of a computer screen. Again, turn off all lights in the sleep room at night including LED clocks, surge protectors or night lights. Many electronic devices have tiny red, blue or green bulbs that stay on and are disruptive in a dark room even when the attached appliances are turned off.

Dentistry is an important healthcare subject that needs to be addressed because it is a field that is directly responsible for great and unnecessary physical, economic, social and environmental pain. Some of its practices continue to be simply barbaric.

The most egregious example of dental barbarism is the long outmoded, continued use of mercury fillings. Mercury is a very dangerous toxin. Period. It should never have been nor continue to be placed in the human body, ever. Do not listen to any rationalizations from anyone supporting its continued use.

Do not ever allow mercury fillings to be placed in teeth. If already present, consider getting them removed as soon as possible.

This cannot be stressed enough. Exposure to mercury damages the body, causes pain, creates economic and other stresses to our medical system, is very hazardous to store and transport and very difficult to clean up.

If plagued by headaches, jaw, neck or shoulder pain, hearing issues, irritability, eye strain, depression, sinus trouble, difficulty concentrating, and a host of other chronic ailments, consider checking with a dentist to see if the teeth are under stress. In particular, see if the teeth are aligning properly and the bite is good. So much of what happens in and to the mouth affects the rest of the body greatly, yet dentistry remains a discipline apart from medicine.

Healthcare costs could be reduced drastically if people took control of their own health and practiced more preventative measures. Learn about the immune system and how it works. Research possible lower-cost and healthier ideas before needing drugs, x-rays or surgery. Work with the body and not against it, and not only will good health be established and maintained, stresses on our healthcare system will be reduced.

On Children

As a society we need to not only stress the importance of feeding our babies breastmilk, we need to support it entirely for at least the first year of development—if not longer. This is a major cultural issue needing drastic improvement. Employers, communities and/or government should not take this issue lightly, because society has suffered and will continue to suffer as ever increasing numbers of children are fed, comforted and entertained artificially. Not only does health suffer, but emotional and developmental problems result when children are detached from the human contact, care and love that breastfeeding provides in the very early days, weeks and months of infants' lives.

Breastfeed babies for at least a year if not longer.

Then, when it comes time to feed baby solids, resist the urge to buy jarred baby food or processed cereals, even of the organic type. Make fresh food in the home and blend it in a small mini-food processor if necessary. Steam veggies and slow cook meats and eggs thoroughly. Avoid cereals, sweets, fish and dairy. Add each food gradually, one at a time. Help the child's palate enjoy vegetables and protein, and then introduce small amounts of natural sweetness, such as berries, rather than the super-sweetness of processed sugars. Have them teethe on sourdough bread crust with a little coconut oil.

Resist the urge to feed growing children mass amounts of altered dairy products. Raw milk yogurt, kefir and cheese may eventually be added when the child is older—at least a year old. Of course, make sure plain, raw, fresh fermented cabbage is introduced at the beginning of a solid food diet in small amounts. Just a little bite or two with every meal is all that is necessary as long as the rest of the diet is otherwise sound.

In addition, just as with adults, children may need supplemental Vitamin D3 in the wintertime. There are several brands now available specifically made for children. However, when there is sunshine, expose children to it—in very small doses at first, but gradually increase the amount in order to help them become acclimated to it. Use common sense and all will be fine.

Another issue upon which parents must decide is that of childhood immunization. This is a very contentious issue on both the pro and con sides, and because of this impossible to discuss fully here. Do some self-research and try to make an informed decision.

Many parents who have become frustrated with belittling, sometimes legal, backlash for questioning this practice have spawned a new compromise movement—increasing the spacing of vaccines rather than following the recommended medical schedule exactly. This seems to be somewhat more acceptable to the medical profession than parents who refuse all vaccines. However, in a free society, if parents decide not to vaccinate their children they should have the right (unless their care is subsidized by taxpayer dollars). It is, after all, a strong immune system that truly protects children and adults from disease. Any other type of "protection" is either non-existent or short-lived.[22]

Children's developing bodies are particularly susceptible to damage from and reaction to toxins, so try to limit exposure as much as possible and raise them with pro- and pre-biotic and organic foods early on. This should not include modern commercial versions of traditionally fermented foods, such as yogurt. Avoid high sugar snacks foods like the plague, and that includes fruit juices.

Also, monitor what young children are exposed to from media. Never let children have a cell phone of their own. Put parental locks on Internet and cable usage. Try not to let any technology become a child's babysitter. Rather, involve them in creative pursuits, brain games and time together as a family. The household and society will be better when these small measures are implemented by our culture.

The prescription for children is really the same for adults: get plenty of rest, exercise, pure water, natural light, nutritious food...and love.

---

[22] Failed vaccination programs happen more often than most people realize. Industry's response to this is to recommend ever increasing frequencies and dosages of drugs and vaccines, just as agribusiness dumps ever increasing amounts of herbicides on our fields. At what point do we realize more is not necessarily better?

On Supplementation

Sometimes taking certain vitamin supplements can be beneficial, but far too often it is a waste of money—and there is a lot of it to be made. Just as with pharmaceuticals, perhaps we are led to believe we need more than we actually do. The truth could be as simple as this:

There is no need to take multivitamins if diet and lifestyle are sound.

However, there is one vitamin that is recommended here that most Americans do not get enough of—Vitamin D3. Rather, most Americans do not get enough sunshine.

Vitamin D3 supplementation is essential for people living in much of the northern two thirds of the United States during the winter season.

In fact, Vitamin D3 should be taken by people living in the northern one third year-round, with perhaps the exception of the height of the short summer season. As most people know by now, this recommendation comes from what scientists almost begrudgingly admit is a serious lack of the heretofore dreaded pure sunshine. Sunshine affects not only Vitamin D levels, but improves our mood, regulates our biorhythms, protects our skin and relieves pain, among other benefits. Try to sunbathe whenever possible. All that is needed is about 15-20 minutes on each side.

Probiotic supplementation can be very useful when a body is under a great deal of stress and higher, immediate doses are required, such as when antibiotics are taken.

Since stress affects our digestion, it makes sense to take supplemental probiotics during times of stress. This can help us maintain levels that in turn help our bodies cope with the damaging effects of stress. Of course, antibiotic use is a major stress on the body and probiotic supplementation is essential in this case, along with consuming fresh foods containing probiotics such as raw fermented cabbage.

On Beauty

Beauty truly does come from within. Sound dietary practices will help keep teeth white, skin beautiful and hair shiny. Relaxation, exercise and happiness also help keep stress from prematurely aging us.

Save a lot of money on personal care products for the teeth by brushing with hydrogen peroxide (H_2O_2) or baking soda instead of toothpaste and swishing with H_2O_2 or coconut oil instead of mouthwash. Add a few drops of pure peppermint or other essential oil if desired. As most people already know, a healthy body will result in healthy teeth. Think about teeth as being more important from the inside out, not the other way around.

Do away with all commercial mouth products and concentrate more on diet to care for teeth.

Skin condition is also dependent upon the condition of the inside of a body. No matter what products are slathered on the surface of skin, the body will attempt to discharge impurities through it. This is how it is supposed to work. Therefore:

Do not use products that block pores from doing their job, such as antiperspirants.

Skin conditions indicate an internal problem. Listen to what the body may be saying and figure out how to work with it. Do not block pores; this will simply force impurities back into the body.

Another beauty tip for fair skinned people is to expose the skin to natural sunshine, rather than slather on creamy chemical cocktails that block the beneficial effects of the it. This may take some time but it can be done little by little. Naturally do not burn the skin, but about 15-20 minutes is all that is ultimately necessary. Build up resistance to burning with 5-10 minutes to begin with, and develop something that everyone agrees makes a fair-skinned person look healthier— an even tan. Avoid tanning salons and opt for natural sunshine whenever and wherever possible.

Most large cosmetic companies' products should be avoided—especially those designed for use around the eyes. Eyes can become irritated and even damaged by some eye makeup. There are often just too many unnecessary and sometimes dangerous substances used in too many personal care products. There are some small companies that produce organic cosmetics and plenty more that have been producing pure soaps and shampoos for quite some time. These products can be more expensive, but using them sparingly can stretch them out and many of them come quite concentrated.[23] In fact, hair should not be washed every day anyway, so stretch out the hair care products by washing less often and letting the body's natural oils moisturize hair. In addition, if covering gray is desired, try using henna or other vegetable-based products.

[23] Think about related costs too that may result from overuse of cosmetic chemicals, such as extra trips to the eye doctor.

Wash hair with organic products no more than once per week.

For skin, natural oils are far less expensive and far better than commercial creams and lotions. A favorite is coconut oil, which can be used on any skin and hair to moisturize. Cleanse with coconut oil too by applying and leaving on for a while before showering, then wash away impurities leaving face and hair shiny, soft and beautiful.

Use coconut and other oils for cleansing and moisturizing instead of commercial chemical concoctions.

Another little secret is that when cooking, if using olive oil, coconut oil, or really any other oil, take the utensils, bowls or pans with the oily residue and smooth into hands, elbows, knees or any other skin. This will not only moisturize, it will save resources in cleaning up.

On Well-Being

Well-being involves a satisfaction with life that is healthy and productive. If human beings need one thing other than basic sustenance, it is meaning and purpose in life. This often comes from establishing good relationships with others, working toward a goal in an enjoyed occupation and spending some time in leisure and relaxation.

Think about relationships with friends, family and other loved ones and how important they are for well-being. These are relationships that are nurtured through understanding, spending time together, helping each other and celebrating life together. During times of trouble, friends and family will be there to assist.

Now think about the friends in our bellies. Our relationship with them needs to be nurtured too, through understanding, protection from harm and supplying them with what they need to stay strong. In return, they will be there to assist us when we need them. Hopefully, this book has helped readers to learn about this important relationship and how it can improve individual and cultural well-being.

May the tiniest among life receive the respect and caring they deserve.

And feel free to share these secrets with others!

The Cabbage Cove...

...is a "micro-cabbagery" offering unique varieties of raw, fresh fermented cabbage that delight the palate and compliment any meal. We strive to use the freshest ingredients possible, preferring organic and/or locally grown produce and herbs when available.

All varieties contain cabbage, purified water and sea salt, in addition to the mixture of ingredients that make each variety so flavorful and unique. Each batch is gluten-free, vegetarian, and low-carb. In addition, the Cabbage Cove takes special orders for any dietary needs or wants, such as allergies or taste preferences.

Cabbage Cove varieties currently available include Cajun, Cinnamon, Garlic & Ginger, Garlic & Herb, German, Ginger & Lime, Greek, Horseradish, Indian, Italian, Japanese, Korean, Lemon Bay, Lemon & Pepper, Mexican, Plain, Spicy, Thai and Ukrainian.

The Cabbage Cove motto is: *"If you like sauerkraut, you're gonna love this stuff. If you don't like sauerkraut, you're gonna love this stuff!"*

Email thecabbagecove@hotmail.com or

Visit the website thecabbagecove.com or

Visit the Facebook page www.facebook.com/thecabbagecove

Share recipes, ask questions or leave comments. Become part of the raw fermented foods movement!

About The Author

Kyla Titus

Kyla spent most of her early life in the neighborhoods of Brooklyn, the beaches on Fire Island and the manicured lawns in Peekskill, New York. She worked as a computer programmer and documentation analyst and writer before deciding to raise her children on her mother's farm in central New York. She also worked in the fields of journalism and special education, and has a bachelor's degree in cultural studies and communications.

During her time on the farm, Kyla decided to raise her children to appreciate and work with the natural world by growing a lot of their own food, making their own things instead of buying them, and, of course, fermenting cabbage.

In an effort to make the ferments more interesting for her children, Kyla experimented with texture and flavor and soon learned that anyone could enjoy this probiotic-rich food, even those who did not like cabbage or traditional sauerkraut. Her mission became sharing her decades of experience in the form of introducing the ferments to the public and speaking and writing about its importance.

Made in the USA
Charleston, SC
02 October 2016